The Little Book of Colour, Shape and Number

Early mathematical experiences

Written by
Clare Beswick

Edited by Sally Featherstone

Illustrations by Sami Sweeten

Little Books with **BIG**ideas®

The Little Book of Colour, Shape and Number
ISBN 1 905019 27 X

© Featherstone Education Ltd, 2005
Text © Clare Beswick, 2005
Series Editor, Sally Featherstone

First published in the UK, July 2005

'Little Books' is a trade mark of Featherstone Education Ltd

The right of Clare Beswick to be identified as the author of this work has been asserted in accordance with Sections 77 and 78 of the Copyright, Designs and Patents Act, 1988.

All rights reserved. No part of this publication may be reproduced by any means, stored in a retrieval system, or transmitted in any form or by any means, electronic, mechanical, photocopying, recording or otherwise, without the prior written consent of the publisher. This book may not be lent, sold, hired out or otherwise disposed of by way of trade in any form of binding or with any cover other than that in which it is published without the prior consent of the publisher, and without this condition being imposed upon the subsequent user.

Published in the United Kingdom by
Featherstone Education Ltd
44 - 46 High Street
Husbands Bosworth
Leicestershire
LE17 6LP

Printed in the UK on paper produced in the European Union from managed, sustainable forests

Contents

Focus of the page	page number
Introduction	4 and 5
Links with the Early Learning Goals	6 and 7
Colour	
It's the same colour	8 and 9
Get sorted	10 and 11
Patterns of colour	12 and 13
Colour games	14 and 15
Mixing colours	16 and 17
Black and white	18 and 19
More spots and stripes	20 and 21
Rainbow colours	22 and 23
Shape	
It's the same shape	24 and 25
Shape names	26 and 27
Corners and sides	28 and 29
Flat shapes and solids	30 and 31
All things round	32 and 33
Tricky triangles	34 and 35
Squares and rectangles	36 and 37
More flat shapes	38 and 39
Number	
One, two, three	40 and 41
Number names	42 and 43
Guess how many	44 and 45
Counting to five	46 and 47
Numbers to ten	48 and 49
Countdown	50 and 51
One more, one less	52 and 53
Writing numerals	54 and 55
Working with parents	56 and 57

The Little Book of Colour, Shape and Number

Introduction

This little book is focused on three aspects of mathematical development, colour, shape and number. It provides fun easy to do activities for children at all stages of the foundation stage and follows on with ease from the competent learner strands of birth to three matters.

The suggested activities offer many opportunities for children to discover and build their mathematical knowledge and develop mathematical language through a wide range of activities which include:

- sand and water play;
- small world play;
- role-play of everyday situations;
- cooking;
- creative activities;
- active play indoors and out;
- games and construction.

Through this range of activities children have the opportunity to learn a number of key skills and concepts, including:
- differentiating colours and shapes;
- matching, sorting and naming colours and shapes;
- describing shapes by their attributes;
- understanding and using size and position language;
- counting to ten, and back to one;
- one to one correspondence;
- counting one more and one less.

They will explore:
- shapes of everyday objects, colours, shapes and numbers in the environment;
- mixing and changing colours;
- patterns of shape and colour;
- flat and solid shapes;
- how shapes fit together;
- guessing and estimating how many;
- mark making and writing numerals for a purpose;
- counting and combining groups of objects.

Children need to be curious, and confident about their mathematical knowledge and language, ready to use what they are learning and discovering to make further discoveries.

All the activities are fun and easy to do, at home as well as in settings, using easily to hand everyday resources. The Little Book is intended for everyone working with children in the foundation stage, in schools, preschool playgroups, nurseries or at home.

The activities are:
- carefully planned to help children make progress towards the early learning goals;
- practical, fun and exciting;
- planned to harness children's natural curiosity;
- easily adapted for children at different developmental stages;
- ideal for small groups or individual children.

The Little Book of Colour, Shape and Number

How the book is written

Each double page spread focuses on specific concepts and skills. There are eight different spreads for each of the three areas covered; colour, shape and number. On each spread, the key words and key skills and concepts being learnt are highlighted, along with clear links to the early learning goals. Ideas for observation and assessment are included and ten great ideas to get you started are provided. For children ready for more, taking it further, provides extension ideas.

Mathematics is fun and a part of our everyday lives. This is an important message to get across to children and parents. Check out the parents' pages at the end of the book for more 'Working together' ideas.

The book addresses many goals for early learning, but its major focus is mathematical development. The goals for mathematics are listed below, but many of the activities also offer opportunities for learning for children who are at an earlier stage of development, and may be working within the stepping stones. On each activity page you will find a mixture of relevant statements from both the stepping stones and the goals.

Early Learning Goals for Mathematics

- say and use number names in order in familiar contexts;
- count reliably up to 10 everyday objects;
- recognise numerals 1-9;
- use developing mathematical ideas and methods to solve practical problems;
- in practical activities and discussion begin to use the vocabulary involved in addition and subtraction;
- use language such as more, less, to compare 2 numbers;
- find one more or one less than a number from 1-10;
- begin to relate addition to combining two groups of objects, and subtraction to taking away;
- use language such as greater, smaller, heavier or lighter to compare quantities;
- use everyday words to describe position;
- talk about, recognise and recreate simple patterns;
- use language such as circle, or bigger to describe the shape and size of solids and flat shapes;
- use developing mathematical ideas and methods to solve practical problems.

It's the same colour

Focus: Matching colours

Steps along the way (stages of development of this concept):

- Matching everyday objects and pictures of everyday objects.
- Matching identical objects of the same colour.
- Matching pictures of the same colour.
- Matching different objects of the same colour.
- Matching red, blue and yellow.
- Matching more colours.

Early Learning Goals:

CLL: use vocabulary focused on objects & people who are of particular importance to them
MD: use mathematical language in play; observe and use positional language
KUW: sort objects by one function
CD: begin to differentiate colours

Key skills and concepts:

- understanding same and different
- identifying attributes

Key words:

* same
* different
* like
* match

The Little Book of Colour, Shape and Number

Ten ideas to get you started:

- Put lots of toy cars in a bucket. Put a red car in the middle of the floor. Pass the bucket around, taking turns to each find a red car to build a 'red car traffic jam' on the floor.
- Use lots of red and yellow balloons. See if the children can tap all the red balloons through a red hoop, the yellow ones through a yellow hoop.
- Chalk a blue line and a green line on the floor, each snaking their way around the setting. Let each child choose a green or blue bit of paper from a box. Children then balance their way along the line matching their paper, before returning for another go.
- Thread red cotton reels onto red laces, green on green. Thread blue ribbon through blue card; thread yellow collage bits onto yellow wool.
- Make colourful place mats for the home corner so that the children can match cups, bowls and spoons to shapes of the same colour.
- Put together a basket of plain coloured gloves, socks and scarves. Play together to find matching pairs.
- Look out for nesting barrel toys. Hide slips of coloured paper in each to match the colour of the barrel.
- Build towers of bricks. Stick red stickers and pictures on the red tower, blue on the blue tower and so on.
- Help the children to tie and stick green objects and pictures on a green hoop. Try and include natural and man made objects, everyday objects as well as some more unusual items. Start to introduce lots of describing words and words to describe different shades of colours.
- Play Kim's memory game with a tray of objects of one colour, such as a yellow sponge, yellow toothbrush, yellow spoon, yellow hat, yellow boot.

Taking it further:

☞ Play 'I spy something that is ....', say 'orange'.

☞ Play musical colours. Dance around to music. When the music stops, call out a colour, eg red, when the children must freeze, orange for them to tiptoe along slowly, green for scurrying.

Look and listen:

- Watch how children compare objects and pictures physically as well as visually.
- Listen to the language they use, and the range of purposes for which they use language.
- Do they understand 'same' and 'different?' Do they use this language in everyday situations?

The Little Book of Colour, Shape and Number

Get sorted

Focus: Sorting by colour

Steps along the way (stages of development of this concept):

- Matching everyday objects of the same colour.
- Matching miniatures that represent familiar objects.
- Sorting a group of the same toys in two colours.
- Sorting objects of three or more colours.
- Sorting pictures by colour.
- Sorting objects according to patterns of colour.

Early Learning Goals:

MD: show an awareness of similarities in shapes in the environment; use everyday words to describe position
KUW: sort objects by one function; notice and comment on patterns
CD: begin to differentiate between colours

Key skills and concepts:

- understanding same and different
- identifying attributes; matching

Key words:

- same
- different
- few
- less
- many
- lots
- more

10 The Little Book of Colour, Shape and Number

Ten ideas to get you started:

- Put together a treasure basket of red and yellow objects to explore. Include some matching pairs of objects. Sit with the children to encourage use of the key words.
- Paint a giant rainbow onto a large sheet of paper (an old roll of wallpaper is ideal). Tear pictures from old magazines and catalogues, sort according to colour and stick onto the matching band of the rainbow.
- Sort a collection of different coloured buttons into ice cube trays.
- Fill plastic bottles with different coloured water. Play at pouring the water into different tiny containers and sorting these by colour, all the red ones here, all the yellow ones here.
- Practise fishing for small coloured bricks with sieves and colanders in the water tray. Sort the bricks found according to colour.
- Sort silver and gold coloured objects, coins and jewellery.
- Make lots of different coloured hand and foot prints and sort them into matching pairs.
- Use some simple balance scales and encourage the children to sort a group of small objects of two colours, all the blue ones in one weighing pan, and all the green in the other.
- Wash and sort coloured plastic cutlery into cutlery trays.
- Sort coloured pieces of collage materials and paper by colour and use them to make jewellery.

Taking it further:

- Sort and explore patterns.
- Put up a washing line and hunt for paper, fabric and objects that can be fixed to the washing line. Choose a theme for each washing line collection, such as all stripes, spots, flowers.

Look and listen:

- Listen to the range of describing words and positional language used.
- Watch to see the strategies they use to compare objects, such as holding them next to other objects, looking, handling the objects etc.
- Look out for examples of sorting and matching skills in everyday situations, such as matching shoes, sorting cutlery and so on.
- Are the children able to sustain their attention and complete tasks?

The Little Book of Colour, Shape and Number

Patterns of colour

Focus: Matching colours

Steps along the way (stages of development of this concept):

- Matching, selecting and naming colours.
- Recognising simple repeating patterns.
- Noticing similarities and differences in everyday objects.
- Following on simple patterns.
- Matching and sorting by pattern.
- Creating own colour patterns; naming simple patterns.

Early Learning Goals:

MD: show awareness of similarities in shapes in the environment; talk about, recognise and recreate simple patterns
KUW: notice & comment on patterns; look closely at similarities, differences, patterns and change
CD: explore colour, texture, shape, form and space in two and three dimensions

Key skills and concepts:

- recognising repeated patterns; same, similar and different
- planning & selecting colours & shapes
- following left to right, and top to bottom

Key words:

* stripes
* checks
* more, again
* end
* zigzags
* circles, round, spots
* beginning
* colour and shape words

Ten ideas to get you started:

- Make simple circle games exploring bags of different patterned fabrics and clothes.
- Plan a spotty or stripey day, inviting children to wear spots or stripes, make patterned badges, hats, paintings and cakes.
- Try making patterns with play dough. Show the children some patterned objects and then try to make your own similar patterns.
- Explore animal patterns. Look for pictures of animals and butterflies with different patterns. Paint your own patterned animals.
- Make printed patterns, or collage and paint stripey patterns.
- Give the home corner a checked, stripey or spots theme. Paint and print tablemats, use some patterned fabric as blankets and curtains and add dressing up clothes in the same pattern.
- Paint repeating patterns on long narrow strips of paper as borders for pictures.
- Use icing pens to create repeating patterns on plain biscuits.
- Chalk patterns outside, make patterned streamers, or create some black and white bunting with paper or fabric squares and triangles in repeating patterns.
- Use gold paint and glitter pens to create sparkling spots, zigzags or stripes on old CDs. Try wax rubbings with silver and gold crayons over coins and glue these to the edge of the disk in repeating patterns.

Taking it further:

☞ Try creating patterns of dark and light tones of the same colour, dark blue, light blue, or perhaps with cars, socks, bricks, buttons, paint spots.

☞ Offer some sponges, potatoes, or other vegetables for printing, and explore patterns of different prints.

Look and listen:

- Listen for key words and for children describing patterns and colours from home.
- Observe how children are able to recall and reproduce patterns.
- Watch children as they experiment with colour and pattern. Consider what is influencing their choices.
- Are the children able to sustain their attention and complete activities?

Colour games

Focus: Matching colours

Steps along the way (stages of development of this concept):
- Differentiating between colours.
- Matching, selecting and naming colours.
- Following simple rules.
- Taking turns, sharing.
- Being part of a group.
- Negotiating, working in pairs.

Early Learning Goals:
CLL: use language for an increasing range of purposes; sustain attentive listening
MD: use mathematical language in play
PD: move with confidence, imagination and in safety

Key skills and concepts:
- recognising and naming colours
- understanding same, similar and different
- following simple rules; taking turns

Key words:
* colour words   * turn
* next   * listen
* words for shades, light, dark, bright
* same, similar, different

14   The Little Book of Colour, Shape and Number

Ten ideas to get you started:

❋ Fix twelve large circles on the floor, three of each colour, starting with red, blue, yellow and green. For older children confident with colour recognition, use secondary colours and shades of the same colours. Give each child a teddy and play some music. Dance around until the music stops, call out a colour and encourage each child to sit their teddy on a circle of that colour!

❋ Share out ball pool balls between children sitting in a circle. Put a large box in the centre on the floor. Call out a colour and the children can throw the balls of that colour into the box.

❋ Sit on the floor in a circle with each child holding a different coloured car. Call out colours randomly. Roll cars of that colour across to the person opposite.

❋ Hide tiny coloured jewels and sequins in a very shallow tray of silver sand. Take turns to hunt for treasure. Give each child a pot for their own treasure. When all the treasure is collected, count how many jewels of each colour each child has found.

❋ Visit the local toy library for lots of colour lotto and domino games.

❋ Give each child a coloured balloon. When their colour is called, the child needs to pat the balloon high in the air and catch it again.

❋ Try a colours treasure hunt. Hide a collection of coloured hats, socks and gloves around the room. Ask the children to work together to find, say a red hat, and then a blue sock.

❋ Play a variation of the shopping memory game, 'My grandmother went to the shops and bought...'. Use a stack of different coloured bricks and choose items according to the colour, such as a red apple, a blue bag and so on. Line up the bricks to prompt recall.

❋ Put a tiny coloured sticky label in the palm of each child's hand. Dance around, when the music stops, point to a child, guess what colour they have and then ask them to hold their hands up so everyone can shout out the colour.

❋ Make a stack of coloured tickets for outdoor play. Create a pay station and every time a child rides, runs or scoots past the pay station, they must pay the ticket collector with a coloured ticket. The child can name the colour or perhaps the ticket master may ask for a specific colour.

Taking it further:

☞ Introduce size words alongside colour words, such as the big red car, the small blue butterfly and so on. Play games of hiding objects and then asking the children to find them describing them by colour as well as size. Encourage position words, such as near, far, high, low, in, on and under.

Mixing colours

Focus: How do colours mix together?

Steps along the way (stages of development of this concept):

- Differentiating between colours.
- Being confident to try new activities.
- Use describing words.
- Predicting.
- Seeking out others to share experiences.
- Exploring change; recording and reporting findings.

Early Learning Goals:

KUW: investigate objects & materials, by using all their senses as appropriate

CD: explore what happens when they mix colour; choose particular colours to use for a purpose; explore colour, texture, shape, form and space in two or three dimensions.

Key skills and concepts:

- recognising, naming, differentiating colours
- understanding same, similar and different
- pouring, mixing, stirring, describing, predicting

Key words:

* float
* mix
* separate
* top/bottom
* sink
* dissolve
* empty/full
* same/different

Ten ideas to get you started:

- Lay a collection of small interesting objects of different colours, textures and shapes on a flat reflective surface, such as foil or a mirror. Try baubles, shells, sequins, shiny buttons, jewellery and so on. View these through layers of tissue, cellophane, transparent fabrics and so on.
- Fill small plastic bottles with water. Carefully add drops of different food colouring or bath oils. Add sequins and glitter. Seal well. Watch the colours mingle and talk about the changes that you see. Watch what happens when you shake the mixture.
- Line a large cardboard box with patches of black paper, foil, bubble wrap and textured wallpaper. Put the box on its side and drape some dark fabric over the entrance to the box. Explore the inside of the box with coloured torches.
- Experiment with making new colours, mixing powder and ready-mix paint. Try to match these to colours on paint colour charts. Use ice cube trays to mix water colour paints to create a palette of new colours.
- Hang up lots of old CDs. Shine different coloured torches on the CDs. Try shining them through fabric, different papers, or holes cut in thick card. What happens when you look at them through sunglasses with different coloured plastic lenses?
- Mix lots of different colours by adding tiny drops of food colouring to water in ice cube trays. Experiment adding tiny quantities of powder paint or brusho to each compartment. Use a plastic dropper to put tiny droplets on different types of paper such as blotting paper, cellophane, tissue.
- Use coloured sand, rice and gravel to make some sand art. Mix the different colours together. Shake up some coloured sand with clear water and then add a few drops of other colourings to see what happens.
- Make some traffic light jellies, or cut open some fruits and vegetables and watch the colours change over time.
- Mix icing sugar and water to make some runny icing. Add tiny amounts of different colours. Spread them one on top of the other. Do the colours mix? What changes can you see?
- Make magic potions, with tiny stirrers in plastic pots and bottles. Start with water but let the children create their own recipes using a selection of ingredients, some of which will dissolve, others that will not mix in. Include a range of wet and dry ingredients. Talk about the colour and other changes that you observe.

Taking it further:

- Think of different ways of recording the changes observed, in pictures, by talking into a tape player, taking photographs, writing labels and diagrams.

Black and white

Focus: colours and counting

Steps along the way (stages of development of this concept):

- Showing an interest in numbers; counting to three by rote.
- Matching and counting one to one.
- Counting to ten; knowing on more and one less.
- Combining objects and numbers to add.
- Taking objects and numbers away to subtract.
- Recognising and counting groups of one, two and three objects.

Early Learning Goals:

MD: say and use number names in order in familiar contexts; count reliably up to ten everyday objects; recognise numerals; use language such as more or less to compare two numbers; find one more or one less than a number from one to ten

Key skills and concepts:

- using mathematical language
- counting; one to one correspondence
- predicting and estimating

Key words:

* number words   * more, less
* few, many   * same
* each

Ten ideas to get you started:

- Practise putting black and white counters or buttons out on a chess or draught board, one on each square, matching the counter to the colour of the square.
- Make some large black and white numerals to make a number line. Try white splatter or bubble painting onto black paper shapes, or white sand glued onto black paper, or black collage or paint on white textured wallpaper and so on. Use the number line to practise counting, finding the number before, and number after.
- Cut black spots from paper and glue to white paper plates. Write the number of spots in marker pen on the back of the plate. Spin the plates, guess how many spots on each plate, count and then turn over to check.
- Make simple paper planes from black and white paper. Add a numeral to each plane. Call out the plane numbers in ascending order, throwing each plane as its number is called. Try this going back from 10 to 1.
- Roll up lots of pairs of black and white socks. Number three buckets or boxes 1, 2, 3. Call out a number and see how many pairs of black socks and how many pairs of white socks you can get in that bucket. See how many pairs altogether.
- Make some black play dough. Write numerals on white paper plates and see if you can roll out and then use a cutter to make the right number of play dough cakes for each plate.
- Blow up black and white balloons. Hang a huge paper holdall or net out of the children's reach. See how many balloons the children can pat into the bag or net. Count how many black balloons, how many white, which is more?
- Make a black and white zebra crossing outside using chalk. Practise crossing, stepping on each colour and counting as you walk, one count for each step. Make a path for hopping, bunny hopping or even walking backwards.
- Make some giant black and white dominoes with white spots on black card.
- Use black and white newsprint to make some interesting pass the parcels. Number each layer. See if the children can guess the contents, perhaps three spoons, six small cars and so on.

Taking it further:

☞ Make some giant black and white dice, with white spots on a black card dice and black spots on a white card dice. Practise matching the numbers of spots to numerals, counting one more and one less, combining the numbers to see how many altogether and perhaps even with objects to help, practise taking away.

More spots and stripes

Focus: colour and construction

Steps along the way (stages of development of this concept):

- Stacking and fitting bricks together.
- Building bridges and stairs.
- Copying patterns and constructions.
- Nesting, sorting and ordering.
- Joining and fixing together.
- Manipulating materials.

Early Learning Goals:

KUW: build and construct with a wide range of objects, selecting appropriate resources and adapting their work where necessary; construct with a purpose in mind, using a variety of resources

CD: explore colour, texture, shape, form and space in two and three dimensions

Key skills and concepts:

- understanding 'same' and 'different'
- identifying attributes of familiar objects

Key words:

- colour and size words
- shape words
- position words, eg high/low
- join, build, strong
- corner, straight

20   The Little Book of Colour, Shape and Number

Ten ideas to get you started:

- Build towers of bricks of one colour, or alternating colours. Try different stripey patterns. Practise turn taking, working in pairs and small groups to take turns to build the towers.
- Create bridges and steps, using different coloured bricks. Add sticky labels, paper and pens to make barcode and domino patterns on the bricks.
- Practise ordering with nesting and stacking toys. Wrap junk boxes in stripey and spotty paper. Stack them and try fitting them into smaller spaces, perhaps in a large box or within an outline on a larger piece of paper.
- Use large sheets of wrapping and wallpaper with stripes and spots, long lengths of ribbon and fabric and huge cardboard boxes for some large-scale construction or den building.
- Create a spots and stripes beach play area. Look out for stripey deckchairs, picnic blankets and a sun umbrella. (make sure the children do not fold the chairs - they could trap fingers!) Make a spots and stripes picnic, perhaps stripes of ham, or thinly sliced cheese, with strawberry fruit spots. Make sunhats from stripey paper.
- Hammer and glue off-cuts of wood together to make boats. Add stripey and spotty fabric or paper sails.
- Decorate a paper plate with spots. Add numerals to make a clock face. Use stripey straws or card for the hands of the clock, fixed with a simple split pin.
- Look at pictures and photographs of stripey and spotty animals. Make some fantasy animals using a wide variety of collage materials. Try to make the animals 3D using different junk boxes.
- Build simple paper kites, from diamond shapes paper, adding stripey and spotty letters to the tail, to spell the child's name.
- Glue stripey and spotty streamers to balloons. Show the children how to pump up the balloons with a simple air pump and then let go. Talk about what is making the balloon fly. What difference do the streamers make?

Taking it further:

- Explore the idea of camouflage with the children. Talk about different colours and camouflage in different environments. Choose an imaginary environment, such as a snowstorm or a dark forest and plan and build a camouflaged den together.

Look and listen:

- Watch how children handle the materials, explore and experiment and build with a purpose.
- Look to see if they are able to maintain their concentration, persevere and complete their task.

Rainbow colours

Focus: colour and creativity

Steps along the way (stages of development of this concept):

- Steps along the way.
- Differentiating colours.
- Responding to and experimenting with colours.
- Imitating actions.
- Joining in with music and dance.
- Use objects as symbols; imaginative play.

Early Learning Goals:

PD: move with confidence imagination and safety; use movement to express feelings; initiate new combinations of movement and gesture in order to express feelings, ideas and experiences

CD: imitate and create movement in response to music; begin to move rhythmically; use their imagination in art and design, music, dance, imaginative and role play and stories

Key skills and concepts:

- understanding representation and symbols
- develop a sequence of activities
- play co-operatively and imaginatively

Key words:

* same
* like
* pair
* different
* match

The Little Book of Colour, Shape and Number

Ten ideas to get you started:

- Collect lots of different coloured ribbons and scarves. Look for different shades of colour and textures as well as colours. Explore the materials together and see how you can make them move, how you can wear them, what they feel like, how they smell, how you feel wrapped up in them. Play different pieces of music and let the children explore the fabrics and listen to the music feeling and responding in the way they feel most appropriate.
- Look at different pictures and images of butterflies. Think about the range of colours and patterns. Look for butterfly inspired jewellery, fabrics and papers, as well as photographs and pictures. Create your own butterflies using a wide range of collage and paint techniques.
- Put together a treasure basket of multi coloured socks, gloves and hats. Look for different textures. Talk about the colours, favourite colours, other places where you might see similar colours.
- Make simple finger puppets, one for each colour of the rainbow, and use these with the 'I Can Sing a Rainbow' song. Sing while the children wave coloured flags or scarves to the rhythm and words of the song.
- Decorate real and improvised musical instruments with multi coloured paper streamers and ribbons. Make this your rainbow band, playing and singing all your favourite colour theme songs.
- Plan an Elmer day. Read Elmer storybooks, create your own patchwork elephant and activities. Make a patchwork of different coloured fruits for snack, with watermelon, kiwi, honeydew melon, tiny slices of orange and so on.
- Look at some sequinned and textured embroidery and tapestry. Recreate your own using sequins, buttons, layers of coloured paper, ribbons and fabric.
- Create your own rainbow, with different colours of handprints. Help each child to add their name to the rainbow on their favourite colour.
- Create a rainbow scrapbook with colour words, picture lists and rhymes. Encourage children to use a wide range of different colour and shade words.
- Use an overhead projector to project different colours onto a wall, using coloured acetates, or coloured pens on clear acetates. Make shadows and explore the colours, putting transparent fabrics against the wall and shining coloured torches against the image.

Taking it further:

- Exploring rhyming words, patterns of words, and sounds, using colour words. Try adding dance movements and actions to the words. R RRRR Red, bouncing on my bed, shaking my head, …. And so on.

It's the same shape

Focus: matching and sorting shapes

Steps along the way (stages of development of this concept):
- Matching identical regular shapes.
- Matching identical irregular shapes.
- Matching, selecting and naming circle, square, triangle.
- Posting shapes.
- Sorting by shape.
- Finding shapes on everyday objects.

Early Learning Goals:
MD: show awareness of similarities in shapes in the environment; begin to talk about the shapes of everyday objects; match some shapes by recognising similarities and orientation

KUW: show an interest in the world in which they live; notice differences in features of the local environment

Key skills and concepts:
- understanding same and different
- visual discrimination
- listening & persevering to complete tasks

Key words:
* same
* circle
* triangle
* rectangle
* different
* square
* diamond
* star

The Little Book of Colour, Shape and Number

Ten ideas to get you started:

- Put together treasure baskets of everyday objects - round, square, rectangle and triangle shapes. Look at, feel and explore the objects. Talk about the shapes and find other objects or shapes that are the same. Tip all the objects out and them sort them back into the baskets.
- Spread some shapes on the floor. Put matching shapes in a bag. Pass the bag round a circle of children, each child taking out a shape and then matching it to a shape in the centre of the circle.
- Practise posting shapes with simple shape sorting toys and posting boxes. Also try making circle, triangle and square holes in a large sheet of paper and practise posting shapes into the matching holes.
- Try lots of different shape threading. Use a single hole punch to make holes in card shapes and thread these onto laces to make single shape threadings - all the circles on one, squares on another.
- Try masking, stencilling, sponge painting and printing with shapes. Talk about the shapes, match and sort as you paint.
- Make sorting shapes more fun by fishing plastic shapes out of bubbly water in the water tray, and collecting them in clear plastic containers.
- Spread lots of shapes on the floor under a parachute. Choose two children at a time to dive under the parachute to find named shapes.
- Gather together real and improvised musical instruments. Look at the different shapes. Sort the instruments by shape. Do all the instruments of the same shape sound the same?
- Hunt the shape. Hide three circles, squares and triangles around the room. Give the children a shape each and ask them to hunt for a hidden matching shape. Continue until all the hidden shapes have been found.
- Chalk circles, squares, triangles and rectangles on the floor. Give each child a bag full of shapes and encourage them to sort their shapes onto the matching chalked shape on the floor.

Taking it further:

☞ Match and sort diamonds, stars, rectangles and other regular shapes. Also try matching and sorting irregular shapes. Encourage the children to draw and cut out their own shapes. Explore how shapes can fit together.

Look and listen:

- Watch how children explore shapes
- Look at the strategies they use to match the shapes, such as looking, trial and error and so on.
- Do they use language to describe shapes in everyday situations?
- Are they consistent in being able to match and sort shapes, or is this an emerging skill?

Shape names

Focus: Matching colours

Steps along the way (stages of development of this concept):

- Exploring and differentiating shapes.
- Matching shapes.
- Selecting named shapes.
- Naming solid shapes.
- Finding and naming shapes in the environment and in everyday objects.
- Naming circle, square, triangle; then more shapes, eg rectangle, diamond, star.

Early Learning Goals:

MD: select a particular named shape; show curiosity and observation by talking about shapes, how they are the same and why some are different; use developing mathematical ideas & methods to solve practical problems

PD: show respect for other children's personal space when playing among them; use one-handed tools and equipment

Key skills and concepts:

- visual discrimination; matching
- understanding shape words
- use a range of everyday objects

Key words:

* circle
* diamond
* sphere
* cuboid
* edge
* square
* rectangle
* pyramid
* side
* triangle
* star
* cube
* corner

The Little Book of Colour, Shape and Number

Ten ideas to get you started:

* Spread out some plastic shapes at the bottom of a slide, slope, or wide tube. Take turns to grab a shape, name it and then run and drop it down the slide. Play at a furious pace, taking turns but moving as quickly as you can.
* Pass a bag of everyday objects around a circle. Invite each child to choose an object, then find and name a shape on the object.
* Play a memory game. Spread some shapes on a tray. Name all the shapes on the tray. Look at them for a few moments, then cover the tray and carefully remove one shape. Which one is missing?
* Use pre-cut shapes to make some shape collage pictures. Encourage the children to try out different ways of combining the shapes to make different pictures and patterns.
* Hammer panel pins into off-cuts of wood. Use elastic bands and wool wrapped around the panel pins to create different shapes. Name and label the shapes with pictures and words.
* Draw around large shapes with a white pen or chalk on dark paper. Then outline the shapes with fingerprints. Again, make picture and word labels for each shape.
* Use light coloured wax crayons on white paper to draw shapes, freehand or around shape blocks or stencils. Wash over the paper with dilute paint for simple wax resist shape pictures.
* Take a trip to the park, supermarket or high street with a shape-shopping list. Look for everyday objects, of all sizes, man-made and natural, that match the shapes on the shopping list. Take some photos of the shapes.
* Practise feeling, describing and guessing the names of shapes in a feely bag. This is a good game for circle time. Try it with flat and solid shapes, or everyday objects of a particular shape.
* Play shape tag. Tuck a short ribbon very lightly into the back of each child's clothing. Choose one child to start the chasing. When they manage to catch a ribbon, the child who has been caught can shout out 'circle', 'square' or 'triangle' and the chaser then has to put the ribbon in a bucket marked with that shape.

Taking it further:

☞ Give children lots of practical experience of handling shapes and matching them to shapes in everyday objects and the environment.

Look and listen:

* Listen for children using shape names in their play.
* Are the children able to describe features of the shape?
* Watch how they explore the shapes and how the shapes can be fitted together or used.

Corners and sides

Focus: exploring shapes

Steps along the way (stages of development of this concept):

- Differentiating shapes.
- Matching, selecting and naming.
- Describing.
- Exploring with senses.
- Using shapes.

Early Learning Goals:

MD: show interest by sustained construction activity or by talking about shapes or arrangements; begin to talk about shapes of everyday objects; adapt shapes and cut material to size; show an awareness of symmetry

KUW: investigate objects and materials by using all their senses as appropriate; talk about what is seen and what is happening

Key skills and concepts:

- visual discrimination; matching
- understanding shape words
- use a range of everyday object and describing words in short phrases

Key words:

* circle
* diamond
* sphere
* cuboid
* edge
* square
* rectangle
* pyramid
* side
* straight
* triangle
* star
* cube
* corner
* curved

The Little Book of Colour, Shape and Number

Ten ideas to get you started:

- Use textured wallpaper to make a shapes line or montage to feel and explore. Include solid shapes by wrapping junk boxes and tubes and other objects with the textured paper.
- Experiment with small solid shapes in clear plastic containers in silver sand. Look at the patterns and shapes created. Talk about how the sand fills the space around the shape. Try this sort of play in wet sand too. Give the children plenty of unhurried time to explore, discover and test out their ideas.
- Lookout for magnet shape building toys - try your local toy library. Look at the way the magnetic balls sit together.
- Draw circles rectangles, triangles diamonds and squares on thick card. Can you use simple wooden blocks to fill the shapes? Try it with Lego or Duplo too.
- Use straws glued to paper to make different shapes. Cut and bend the straws to make more shapes.
- Count corners and sides on flat shapes and regularly shaped everyday objects.
- Look at how shapes fit inside each other - try eggs in egg boxes, cheese triangles in a round box, sugar cubes in a box, straws in a cylinder, apples on a plate. Talk about corners and edges, spaces between shapes.
- Chalk the outline of huge shapes outside. Practise balancing along the edges, jumping on the corners and so on.
- Draw round and cut out regular shapes. Colour the corners and make patterns along the edges. Practise folding the shapes in half. What new shapes can the children make?
- Roll out play dough and use simple cutters and a plastic pastry wheel to make shapes. Make as many different shapes as possible. Sort them according to the number of corners.

Taking it further:

☞ Put together a treasure basket of natural objects of different shapes. Explore and talk about the shapes together. Talk about straight edges and curves, soft shapes and spikey shapes. Introduce size and length words. Encourage the children to talk about similarities and differences and changes in shape.

Look and listen:

- Listen for children using shape names in their play.
- Are the children able to describe features of the shape?
- Look at how they explore the shapes and how the shapes can be fitted together or used.
- Listen for questions that explore how shape affects how an object behaves or is used.

The Little Book of Colour, Shape and Number

Flat shapes and solids

Focus: exploring shape in two and three dimensions

Steps along the way (stages of development of this concept):

- Finding out about shapes in everyday objects and the environment.
- Differentiating shapes.
- Matching, selecting and naming flat shapes.
- Exploring solid shapes.
- Using words to describe flat shapes and solids.
- Naming simple solids, such as sphere, or cube.

Early Learning Goals:

MD: use language such as 'circle' or 'bigger' to describe the shape & size of solids and flat shapes; use developing mathematical ideas & methods to solve practical problems

KUW: build & construct with a wide range of objects, selecting appropriate resources & adapt their work where necessary; select the tools & techniques they need to shape, assemble & join materials they are using

Key skills and concepts:

- visual discrimination; matching
- understanding shape words
- use a range of everyday object and describing words in short phrases

Key words:

circle	square	triangle
diamond	rectangle	star
sphere	pyramid	cube
side	corner	edge

The Little Book of Colour, Shape and Number

Ten ideas to get you started:

- Use cut out cardboard shapes and small junk boxes and tubes to create simple flat and solid object mobiles.
- Roll up flat rectangles of card and fix with sticky tape to make tubes. Add circles to the ends to make cylinders. Find and talk about other cylinders in your setting.
- Use small junk boxes, glue and paint to make some caterpillars. Collage with flat shapes to make beautiful butterflies. Talk about the differences and similarities between the solid and flat shapes.
- Try some simple woodwork, glueing and nailing tiny flat and solid shapes of wood onto a base.
- Make some padded shapes. Cut large simple shapes and fix to card, stuffing layers of newspaper between the shape and the card.
- Create a shape number line, using flat and solid shapes, such as one triangle, two cubes, three circles, four cylinders etc.
- Try simple moulds in wet sand. Talk about the different flat and solid shapes that can be made or drawn in the sand.
- Make a montage of solid and flat shapes. Display with everyday objects with simple regular shapes, together with shape sorting and posting toys.
- Use a simple bread mix to make some bread dough. Roll out some flat shapes and leave to rise. Talk about how the shapes have changed.
- Use simple construction toys to make a collection of solid and flat shapes.

Taking it further:

- Try rolling and stacking different solid shapes. Encourage the children to predict what might happen, how each shape might behave.

Look and listen:

- Listen for children using shape words and describing objects and features by the shape.
- Look at how children explore the shapes and experiment with how they fit together.
- Watch how they find similarities and differences between the shapes.

All things round

Focus: circles, ovals, cylinders and spheres

Steps along the way (stages of development of this concept):

- Differentiating shapes.
- Matching and sorting round shapes.
- Finding out about straights and curves.
- Exploring rolling.
- Naming round shapes.

Early Learning Goals:

MD: begin to use mathematical names for solid 3D shapes & flat 2D shapes & mathematical terms to describe shapes

KUW: look closely at similarities, differences, patterns and change; ask questions why things happen and how things work

CD: explore colour, texture, shape, form and space in two and three dimensions

Key skills and concepts:

- visual discrimination
- matching, comparing and sorting
- understanding and using shape words
- describing attributes; exploring, predicting

Key words:

* circle
* ball
* tube
* curve
* sphere
* oval
* cylinder
* smooth
* round
* egg
* edge
* flat

32 The Little Book of Colour, Shape and Number

Ten ideas to get you started:

- Use a ball of dough and some straws to make spheres. Stick lots of short lengths of straws into the dough ball to make a spiky ball.
- Explore other ways of making flat and solid round shapes using dough and straws.
- Draw and cut around a flat circle and oval shape. Pierce the centre with a small stick, or blunt end cocktail stick to make spinners. Experiment with the spinners, comparing how they work. Try different patterns on the spinners.
- Gather together lots of different tubes. Try fitting them together, nesting them, stacking short tubes in longer tubes. Experiment with rolling the tubes. Which will roll the furthest? Try this on different surfaces and slopes. What happens if you fill the tubes?
- Collect a wide range of different balls, from tiny plastic balls, ping-pong balls, tennis balls, beach balls, and so on. Include balls with holes and try and get some really heavy balls, such as a bowling ball or boules, as well as some huge balls, perhaps an exercise ball or space hopper.
- Try lots of different rolling experiments. Sort balls and tubes according to size. Feel the different weights. Encourage the children to guess and predict and talk about the shapes. Think about what all the balls have in common and their differences.
- Try making lots of different bubbles. What shape are all the bubbles?
- Hard-boil some eggs. Paint patterns on the eggs and then try rolling and spinning the eggs. Chalk a target area on the floor and see if you can roll the eggs to land on the target.
- Line tin lids and shallow trays with paper. Roll marbles dipped in paint around the trays and lids. Talk about the different patterns and straight lines the spheres have made.
- Create a circles treasure basket of everyday objects, including a ball, penny, CD, pebble, button, orange, round sponge and so on. Try to include objects with different smells and textures, as well as flat and solid objects.

Taking it further:

☞ Look at a globe and pictures of planets. Papier-mâché together over balloons or beach balls to make your own planets. Collage and paint the planets and hang from the ceiling with stars printed onto black paper to make the night sky.

Look and listen:

- Listen for children using shape words and finding these shapes in everyday objects and the environment.
- Observe the strategies they use to match, compare and sort the shapes.

Tricky triangles

Focus: fitting shapes together

Steps along the way (stages of development of this concept):

- Differentiating shapes.
- Counting corners and sides.
- Matching, selecting, sorting and naming triangles.
- Selecting and using shapes for a purpose.
- Exploring how shapes fit together.

Early Learning Goals:

MD: use developing mathematical ideas and methods to solve practical problems; use appropriate shapes to make models or pictures
KUW: look closely at similarities, differences, patterns & change
PD: Handle tools, objects, and malleable materials safely
CD: explore colour, texture, shape and form in two or three dimensions

Key skills and concepts:

- visual discrimination
- matching, comparing & sorting; describing attributes
- handling, joining, placing and fitting together
- awareness of position and orientation

Key words:

* triangle
* edge
* fat
* small
* corner
* sharp
* thin
* side
* point
* large

The Little Book of Colour, Shape and Number

Ten ideas to get you started:

- Cut out large circles and add collage with pictures cut and torn from food magazines and brochures to make pizzas. Use a ruler and marker pen to cut the pizza into triangles. Cut along these lines and play at sharing out the pizza between the members of the group.
- Make a display of triangular shaped boxes, pictures, shapes and objects. Try to include everyday objects and packaging as well as resources from around the setting. Encourage children to bring in objects and pictures from home.
- Try printing and collage onto triangles of different textured paper and card.
- Cut a large piece of stretchy fabric into large triangles. Spread these on the floor and ask a child to hold each corner. Pull the triangles tight. Chant 'Tri-an-gle, 1,2,3, corners and sides, 1,2,3, Tri-an-gle' and on the final word let the fabric go with a ping!
- Cut lots of different sizes and shapes of triangles (tall thin ones, some with sides all the same length, some with right angle corners) from coloured sticky paper and other suitable collage materials. Use these to make pictures and patterns on larger pieces of triangle paper. Print a triangles border.
- Make some triangular treats. Cut triangles from slices of cheese and ham.
- Cut pineapple cubes in half to make pineapple pyramids. Cut slices of melon into triangles.
- Use triangles of cheese spread and triangles of bread to make some cheesy triangles for snack time.
- Cut lots of triangle shapes from thick card, corrugated card, fabric. Use upturned egg boxes and trays with the cut triangles, paint and glue to create some spiky monsters.
- Cut lots of black and white triangles, print onto these with triangles and then tape together to make some triangle bunting.

Taking it further:

☞ Start to explore pyramids, with square and triangle bases. Count the faces of the solid shapes and look at the shape of each face. Try counting the corners too.

Look and listen:

- Listen and check that children understand the names of shapes.
- Watch children sorting the different sorts and sizes of triangles.

Squares and rectangles

Focus: matching colours

Steps along the way (stages of development of this concept):

- Differentiating shapes.
- Counting corners and sides.
- Matching, selecting, sorting squares and rectangles.
- Comparing short and long sides.
- Using describing words for attributes.

Early Learning Goals:

MD: begin to talk about the shape of everyday objects; use shapes appropriately for tasks; observe and use positional language, talk about, recognise and recreate patterns

PD: use one handed tools and equipment; handle tools, objects, constructions and malleable materials safely and with increasing control

Key skills and concepts:

- visual discrimination; describing attributes
- matching, comparing, sorting and ordering
- handling, joining, placing and fitting together
- awareness of position and orientation

Key words:

* same/different
* square
* side
* long/short
* rectangle
* corner

The Little Book of Colour, Shape and Number

Ten ideas to get you started:

- Make a simple letterbox for the home corner. Make square and rectangle postcards to post. Fold some rectangles in half to make square greetings cards. Talk about the shapes of the card.
- Cut very long thin rectangles and some squares. Try folding, rolling and curling the shapes to make different shapes. Use these shapes to collage onto some white textured wallpaper. Look out for paper with regular shapes or relief or textured patterns.
- Use pages from old magazines and pictures pasted to thin card. Cut each into rectangles and squares to make some simple puzzles. Try this with the children's own pictures too.
- Print your own wrapping paper with square and rectangle shapes and then wrap up squares and rectangles.
- Chalk some giant squares and rectangles on the floor. Play a game of jumping, hopping and skipping to different shapes that you call out. Can they stand on a long side, a corner or a short edge?
- Build tall towers with wooden blocks. Try a tower just of cubes, and another of cuboids and some using both shapes of brick.
- Look at some brickwork and see how the bricks are arranged so the joins are staggered in brick bond. Tape a very large sheet of paper to a wall and use square and rectangle shape sponges to print your own brickwork.
- Play Jenga!
- Paint small black and white triangles next to each other to make zebra crossings for the road mat, small cars and play people.
- Use strips of thin card, sticky tape, scissors and cellophane to make your own square and rectangle windows.

Taking it further:

☞ Collect a range of everyday objects that are square or rectangle shape. Sort these into squares and rectangles and then work together to order by size and then by weight.

Look and listen:

- Listen for the children using length, position and shape words in their everyday play and routines.
- Look at how they plan and negotiate their activities.
- Watch how they compare and fit the shapes together.

More flat shapes

Focus: large and small

Steps along the way (stages of development of this concept):

- Understanding large and small.
- Recognising, naming, differentiating shapes.
- Ordering objects by size.
- Ordering shapes by size.
- Using size and position words.

Early Learning Goals:

MD: show curiosity & observation by talking about shapes, how they are the same or why some are different; order two items by height or length; begin to use mathematical names for solid 3D shapes & flat 2D shapes & mathematical terms to describe shapes

PD: handle tools, objects, construction and malleable materials safely and with increasing control

Key skills and concepts:

- visual discrimination
- matching, comparing, sorting and ordering
- describing attributes
- awareness of position and orientation

Key words:

* same   * different   * large
* larger   * largest   * small
* smaller   * smallest   * big
* little   * middle size

Ten ideas to get you started:

- Make a collection of tiny shapes to explore; shells buttons, sequins, tiny card shapes, seeds. Use magnifying lenses and small sieves to search for different shapes. Sort and talk about the shapes, using position, size and shape words.
- Use tiny zip lock bags to make collections of tiny shapes and objects.
- Spread large and small card or plastic shapes (circles, squares, diamonds, rectangles, triangles, stars and ovals) on the floor under a parachute or large sheet. Waft the parachute up and down chanting, 'Lots of shapes, 1,2,3, large and small, large and small, can (name) find .....(pause) a small triangle?' Take turns to dive under the parachute to find the right shape
- Make a shape number line together, one circle, two stars, three triangles etc.
- Make some textured shapes and include the number as well as the shapes.
- Draw and cut out large and small circles. Mark a spiral on each circle and help the children to cut along the spiral line, to make their own spiral puzzles.
- Chalk large and small shapes on the floor. Take turns to throw beanbags towards specified targets, such as the small circle, or the large square and so on. Give the children turns at choosing targets for each other.
- Find a large cardboard tube or length of clean plastic guttering down-pipe. Decorate the tube with different shapes. Take turns to post different shapes down the tube, naming and describing the shape before posting it, eg a large red oval.
- Practise threading pre-cut shapes onto wool or ribbon. Use a single hole-punch to make the threading holes. Try to create patterns of shapes, large, small; or perhaps, large triangle, small circle, large triangle, small circle. Talk about the colour, shape and size of each as you thread and create patterns.
- Make a picture list with the children of familiar everyday objects that are large circles, small circles, large triangles, small triangles, large squares and small squares. Use this to help the children to create their own shapes rhyme, using a simple format or nursery rhyme.

Taking it further:

☞ Practise finding and naming shapes described by the number of corners, sides or other attributes, such as can you find/name a shape with four sides and is the same shape as something on the front door?

Look and listen:

- Listen for the children using size and shape words in their everyday play and routines.
- Watch how they compare shapes. Are they using trial & error or visually scanning shapes to make comparisons?
- Are they able to order groups of the same and different shapes by size?

One, two, three

Focus: first number names and counting

Steps along the way (stages of development of this concept):
- Enjoying anticipation games (ready, steady, go).
- Imitating actions and words.
- Understanding first words and short phrases.
- Using first words and phrases.
- Showing an interest in numbers and counting.

Early Learning Goals:
MD: show an interest in numbers & counting; use some number names & number language spontaneously; enjoy joining in with number rhymes & songs; use mathematical language in play
PD: show respect for other children's personal space when moving among them; move with control & co-ordination

Key skills and concepts:
- imitating actions and words
- recognising number names
- knowing number words have a special importance

Key words:
* ready, steady go
* one, two, three
* now
* wait
* your turn, my turn

The Little Book of Colour, Shape and Number

Ten ideas to get you started:

- Play lots of clapping and stamping games, counting 1,2,3, and 'Ready, steady, go' to a steady beat. Make the games different using different voices and adding in other actions for the child to imitate and count.
- Finger and number rhymes are an ideal way to introduce number names to the youngest children, such as round and round the garden, two little dickey birds and so on. See the end of the book for more number rhymes.
- Blow bubbles and encourage children to count and point to three bubbles before popping one, two three bubbles.
- Roll and cut play dough into round buns. Add buttons as cherries, counting one two three, over and over again. Sing 'Three Currant Buns in the Baker's Shop'.
- Slide teddies down a slide. Count 1,2,3 as you put three teddies on the slide and say 'Ready steady go,' before they are released down the slide.
- Fill shoe boxes with three small balls or rolled up pairs of socks. Hold the boxes low down and together, shout 1,2,3 and then throw the balls in the air. Count three back into each box.
- Blow squares of tissue paper, feathers or chiffon scarves across the room. Count together 1,2,3 before blowing all together.
- Use a steady beat on a drum to count 1,2,3, and then strike a chime bar. Repeat with the children counting and playing instruments. Try it with improvised instruments such as two wooden bricks, sticks or metal spoons.
- Slide cars down a slope, counting to three together before releasing each car in turn or together.
- Make race tracks in the garden and have a Sports afternoon.

Taking it further:

☞ Extend all these activities, by adding position words, or by introducing first counting, matching one object or action to each count (one to one correspondence)

Look and listen:
- Listen for 'Ready steady go', and 1,2,3, being used spontaneously in play.
- Watch for children imitating actions and words and joining in simple rhymes and action songs.
- Look to see if they show an interest in numbers or pretend to count in imitation of adults or other children.

Number names

Focus: using number names in everyday play

Steps along the way (stages of development of this concept):

- Showing an interest in number names.
- Recognising number names.
- First counting, sorting and matching.
- Using numbers in exploring and describing.
- Simple pretend play; building sequences of simple pretend play.
- Using numbers in pretend play.

Early Learning Goals:

CLL: extend their vocabulary, exploring the meaning and sounds of new words; use language for an increasing range of purposes

MD: say and use number names in order in familiar contexts; recognise numerals one to nine; use some number names accurately in play; recognise some numerals of personal significance

CD: engage in imaginative and role-play

Key skills and concepts:

- counting in imitation to three, five or ten
- recognising number names to three, five or ten
- showing an interest in numerals
- recognising numerals to ten

Key words:

* number names
* count
* more
* how many?
* less

Ten ideas to get you started:

- Make shop play a regular feature inside and outdoors. Keep the shops simple but add different props each time. Provide opportunities for mark making with price labels and receipts. Add a till, calculators and telephones.
- Create a simple telephone play area, with lists of telephone numbers, directories and yellow pages, as well as phones. Be sure to include pretend mobile phones as well as more conventional but contemporary phones.
- Make counting and number names a part of baking. Count spoonfuls, cupfuls and so on. Count how many items you have made. Sing simple songs, commentaries and chants emphasising the number names.
- Add number names to familiar songs and rhymes, such as The Wheels on the Bus ..... 'the driver on the bus says 5pence please', or perhaps, 'three babies on the bus went waa, waa, waah!'
- Put some electronic weighing scales in the home corner. Add pens and notebooks for mark making and recording weights.
- Make some pretend front doors with letterboxes, perhaps using large sheets of card, or cardboard boxes. Paint the doors and add house numbers. Make lots of cards with matching numbers to post through the matching letterboxes, or post lots of picture cards through each letterbox, counting them as they are posted.
- Look at and talk about numbers on clocks. Play 'What's the time Mr. Wolf?', emphasising the number names and encouraging children to take turns to shout out the numbers.
- Make number names a part of outdoor play. Make number plates for bikes and pedal cars. Count steps and ladder rungs on the slide and climbing frame.
- Chalk numerals on the floor and call out number names as the children jump from numeral to numeral. Paint a simple hopscotch on the floor.
- Make and number paper boats blowing them across shallow trays.

Taking it further:

☞ Sort groups of objects and count and match the groups to numerals. Practise number names, making numerals in all different media and sorts of textures. Try numbers in wet sand, dribbles of paint, water, or collage numerals in sandpaper, textured wallpaper, bubble wrap, fur fabric.

Look and listen:

- Listen for number names imitated in everyday situations, such as counting together with a practitioner.
- Listen for number names used spontaneously in activities and in simple pretend play.
- Look for children using one to one correspondence.

Guess how many

Focus: guessing to estimate and predict

Steps along the way (stages of development of this concept):

Being confident to guess how many from other clues when they cannot see the group of objects.

Early Learning Goals:

MD: Say & use number names in order in context; count reliably up to ten everyday objects; use developing mathematical ideas & methods to solve practical problems; compare two groups of objects saying when they have the same number; use language such as more or less to compare two numbers

PD: manipulate materials & objects by picking up, releasing, arranging, threading & posting them

Key skills and concepts:

- one to one correspondence
- counting to ten
- guessing and estimating in play

Key words:

- number names
- guess
- count
- many/few
- how many?
- estimate
- lots
- more/less

44 The Little Book of Colour, Shape and Number

Ten ideas to get you started:

- Pan for gold, using sieves and some coloured gravel, glass beads and sequins in a water tray. Guess how many nuggets or gems are in each sieve. Check by counting.
- Use cups and plastic bottles and other clear containers in the sand tray. Guess how many cups of sand are needed to fill the container. Check it out. Try this with spoons of salt and tiny pots, or other materials.
- Fill a large cardboard box with balloons. Can you guess how many balloons are in the box? Now fill it with balls, teddies, clothes and so on.
- Fill a basket with letters or books. Sort them into piles and then guess how many are in each pile.
- Chalk a target onto the centre of a shallow tray. Have three marbles each. Take turns to roll the marbles at the target. Guess how many will be in the target area at the end of the game!
- Use a simple balance scale, with pebbles, shells, corks and cones. Play together talking about and estimating how many objects are needed in each pan to balance the scales.
- Play with the train set. Guess how many trains will fit in a tunnel, how many bricks are needed to build a bridge, how many coaches a train can pull, how many passengers are waiting at the station. Count toy cars into a bucket.
- In the home corner, guess how many teddies are in bed, how many cups are in the cupboard, how many pots on the cooker and so on. Practise estimating how many cups, spoons and plates you need for a dolls tea party.
- Put pennies, sequins and jewels in purses. Can you guess how many is in each purse, which has many and which has just a few?
- Build towers of bricks and guess how many bricks were needed to build the towers. Build wide and narrow towers and guess again.

Taking it further:

- Practise guessing which is the greatest number, which is the fewest. Practise looking and estimating both seen and unseen so that the children are feeling and predicting too.

Look and listen:

- Listen for number names used in everyday situations, and spontaneously in play.
- Watch to see children are using one to one correspondence.
- Look for children making reasonable estimates when they can see the objects to be counted.
- Watch for evidence of increasing confidence with number and wider use of mathematical language.

The Little Book of Colour, Shape and Number

Counting to five

Focus: counting one-to-one to five

Steps along the way (stages of development of this concept):

- Counting together and counting in imitation to three and then to five.
- Knowing the number names to five.
- Using number names to five spontaneously in play and everyday situations.
- Making one count to one number (one to one correspondence).
- Recognising numerals to five.
- Counting independently and consistently groups of up to five objects.

Early Learning Goals:

MD: recognise numerals 1 to 5, then 1 to 10; count out up to six objects from a larger group; select the correct numeral to represent 1 to 5, then 1 to 10; count actions or objects that cannot be moved; use language such as more or less to compare two numbers

Key skills and concepts:

- one to one correspondence
- counting to ten
- using mathematical language in play

Key words:

* each
* different
* less
* number names to ten
* same
* more

The Little Book of Colour, Shape and Number

Ten ideas to get you started:

- Use five each of different colours of small bricks or buttons. Bury these in silver sand. Hunt for all the bricks or buttons, sort and count them together.
- Hold hands in a row and step and count together. Try giant strides, tip toes, jumps, stepping backwards, skipping sideways and so on.
- Collect five small shells, five buttons, five pennies and five sequins, or any other combination of groups of five small objects. Muddle the objects up, sort them into groups and then place each item one at a time in a section of an ice cube tray or other suitable sorting tray, counting carefully 'One count to one object' to five.
- Have five hats, five blankets and five necklaces for five teddies. Dress the teddies, talk about and count the objects. Sit the five teddies in a row and sing to the tune of Ten Green Bottles 'Five Smart Teddies Sitting on a Wall'. At each verse count the teddies carefully, touching each teddy to emphasise one count for each teddy.
- Count and strike chime bars, triangles, drums or piano keys together.
- Wash and dry, sort and count five cups, five spoons, five plates and so on.
- Number and action rhymes are an ideal way of practising counting and one to one correspondence.
- Play shop with each item being priced five pence. Make lots of pretend card pennies. Count out five pence from purses and pockets to make each purchase.
- Make lots of tickets for riders of bikes and scooters outside. Create a simple ticket booth with a table, telephone, mark-making and collection box. Ask each rider to pay five tickets each time they pass the ticket booth.
- Chalk a number line to five on the floor. Jump along the line, one jump per number, jumping and saying the numbers together. Try hopping or bunny hopping along the line. Prompt the children to think of other ways of moving down the number line.

Taking it further:

- Try counting up to five and down from five to zero. Practise finding the number before and the number after a number between one and five.

Look and listen:

- Listen for number names used in everyday situations, and spontaneously in play.
- Watch to see children are using one to one correspondence.
- Watch to see if the children can reliably count five everyday objects.
- Watch for evidence of increasing confidence with number and wider use of mathematical language.

The Little Book of Colour, Shape and Number

Numbers to ten

Focus: counting and recognising numerals

Steps along the way (stages of development of this concept):

- Show an interest in number and use number names in play and everyday situations.
- Counting together and counting in imitation to three, five and then to ten.
- Using number names spontaneously in play and everyday situations.
- Making one count to one number (one to one correspondence).
- Recognising numerals to five, then to ten.
- Counting independently and consistently groups of up to five objects.

Early Learning Goals:

MD: say and use number names in order in familiar contexts; count reliably up to ten everyday objects; recognise numerals 1 to 9

PD: move with confidence, imagination and in safety; show respect for other children's personal space when playing among them

Key skills and concepts:

- visual discrimination
- one to one correspondence
- listening and attention skills

Key words:

* more
* lots
* same
* less
* few
* different

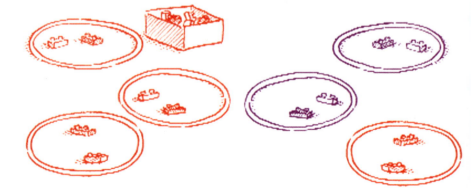

48 The Little Book of Colour, Shape and Number

Ten ideas to get you started:

- Add a little sand to ten large plastic bottles and seal. Label clearly with the numbers one to ten. Play skittles, calling out the number of the bottle knocked down.
- Put tiny sticky labels with the numbers one to ten gently on fingers. Play at pointing with twos, tapping with fives, scratching heads with sevens and so on!
- Use a pile of socks, push on pegs and a low clothesline. Help each child to choose a numbered card from one to ten and then peg that number of socks on their stretch of the line.
- Play hopscotch, calling out the numbers as you hop and jump on each numeral.
- Mark ten squares, in a row on plain paper. Add several more rows of ten squares below. Play at stamping and printing in each square, making patterns and counting to ten along each row.
- Explore computer keyboards, weighing scales, clocks, calculators and telephones pressing different numbers.
- Build a Lego carpark for up to ten cars. Use sticky labels to number each space. Number small cars with sticky labels and park a matching car in each parking space.
- Chalk ten coloured circles on the floor. Label each circle with a number from one to ten. Practise throwing beanbags at each circle. Call out the numbers of the circle each beanbag lands on. Count the number of beanbags on each circle.
- Hide a number of jewels, pennies and shiny buttons in purses and tiny boxes. Count the number of objects in each box and match this to a number on a card.
- Label lots of ball pool balls, one to ten. Throw them all in a large tray or paddling pool. Choose a number and hunt for, say all the twos! Try to find one of each number and put the balls in order.

Taking it further:

☞ Practise putting the numerals in order. Encourage children to use 'First, second, third' as well as the number names. Practise spotting errors, perhaps putting two numbers the wrong way round, or miscounting spots on a dice and so on.

Look and listen:

- Listen for children joining in with counting, using number names in play and counting independently.
- Watch for children recognising numerals of special significance to them, such as their age or house number.
- Check that children can consistently count groups of objects as well as count spots on dice.

The Little Book of Colour, Shape and Number

Countdown

Focus: Gaining confidence with numbers

Steps along the way (stages of development of this concept):

- Using number names in play and everyday situations.
- Counting together and counting in imitation.
- Making one count to one number (one to one correspondence).
- Counting independently groups of objects.
- Recognising numerals to ten.
- Counting forwards and backwards; filling in the missing number.

Early Learning Goals:

MD: count reliably up to ten everyday objects; show an interest in number problems; use language such as more or less to compare two numbers; find one more or one less than a number from one to ten

CD: join in favourite songs; begin to build a repertoire of songs; engage in imaginative and role-play based on their own first hand experiences

Key skills and concepts:

- demonstrate confidence with number
- one to one correspondence
- recognise numerals
- count from one to ten & from ten back to one

Key words:

* number words
* less
* down
* back

* more
* up
* on

The Little Book of Colour, Shape and Number

Ten ideas to get you started:

- Build rockets from junk boxes and decorate with numerals. Cover a table with foil to make a launch pad and count down from ten to one for blast off!
- Familiar rhymes are a great way to count in imitation, count together and learn to count down. Try Ten Green Bottles, Five Elephants Went out to Play, Five Fat Sausages Sizzling in the Pan and Five Currant Buns in the Baker's Shop. There are many more. Look in the Little Book of Nursery Rhymes or use the list at the end of this book.
- Number some cars with sticky labels and race them around a racetrack. Can you line them up in order, or perhaps start with ten and work back to one.
- Play and sing 'Ten in the Bed' with teddies and soft toys in the home corner, or with children under a blanket.
- Put together a numbers treasure basket to explore and talk about. Include clocks, calculators, rulers, mobile phones, and much more.
- Number ping-pong balls with a waterproof marker pen. Practise sorting, counting and ordering the numbered balls as they float in the water tray.
- Tie number labels securely to hoops. Spin the hoops to see which numbered hoop spins the longest. Try rolling the hoops and practise ordering them.
- Add sticky labels to number wooden bricks and see if you can build towers with the numbers in the right order. Count the bricks of the towers together. Count up from the bottom to the top, one to ten and back down to one again.
- Make a sailing regatta in the water tray! Use paper boats or plastic boats. Number the sails. See if you can arrange the boats in order.
- Create number bunting. Paint or collage numbers onto each flag and then arrange the flags in order to create number bunting. Practise counting along the bunting, one to ten and back down from ten to one.

Taking it further:

☞ Provide lots of opportunities for children to try writing numbers in role-play. Provide plenty of different sorts of mark makers, books, paper, white boards.

Look and listen:

- Listen for children joining in with counting, using number names in play and counting independently.
- Check that children can consistently count groups of the same object as well as irregular arrangements of objects.
- Watch to see if the children can reliably match the number of objects they have counted to the numeral.

The Little Book of Colour, Shape and Number

One more, one less

Focus: Towards addition and subtraction

Steps along the way (stages of development of this concept):

- Using number names in play and everyday situations; counting together.
- Making one count to one number (one to one correspondence).
- Counting confidently; recognising numerals to ten.
- Counting forwards and backwards; filling in the missing number.
- Saying the number one more and one less.
- Combining groups and numbers, taking away from groups and numbers.

Early Learning Goals:

MD: count reliably up to ten everyday objects; show an interest in number problems; use language such as more or less to compare two numbers; find one more or one less than a number from one to ten: find the total number of items in two groups by counting all of them; begin to relate addition to combining tow groups of objects and subtraction to taking away

Key skills and concepts:

- count to ten with confidence
- one to one correspondence
- recognise numerals
- find one more and one less than a given number to ten

Key words:

* number words * add
* more   * less
* together   * subtract
* take away

The Little Book of Colour, Shape and Number

Ten ideas to get you started:

- Number and race some cars. Say the number one more and one less than the number of the winner. Order the cars on the start line.
- Make small flags using straws as flagpoles and paper as the flag itself. Make flags one to ten. Arrange the flags in order poking the flagpoles through a box lid. Talk about the flags and play at finding the number one less than, one more than a particular flag.
- Make themed number lines, such as jungle animals, buildings, vehicles, fruit etc. Use the number lines to find the number less than and the number one more than. Match the numerals on the number line to groups of matching objects.
- Use a draught board and different coloured counters. Grab a hand full of counters and sort them by colour into rows, one counter per square. Count how many counters there are of each colour. Which has the most, which has the fewest. What would happen if you combined colours?
- Draw and cut out stars from black and white paper and glue to old CDs. Cover the back of the CDs. Count the number of stars on each CD and write the numeral on the back. Play games ordering the CDs looking at the stars and then turning them all over to check the order of the numerals.
- Put price labels on some play food and grocery boxes. Say the number greater and the number less than each item.
- Use spotty <u>and</u> number dice alone or together. Roll a number dice and say the number one more and the number one less. Roll spotty dice and do the same. Roll two dice and say how many altogether.
- Play with spotty dominoes. Match the number of spots to numerals. Count the spots and say the number less than and the number greater than. Talk about how many more on one end of a domino than the other end.
- Make some number dominoes and play at matching the numerals, finding the right number of counters to match the numerals, as well as saying the number less than and the number greater than.
- Sort coins and arrange in groups. Count each group and say the number less than and the number more than. Combine two groups and say how many altogether. Take one, two or three away from a group and see how many are left. Match the number of coins in the groups to numerals.

Look and listen:
- Listen for children using number names in play and counting independently.
- Check that children can consistently count groups of the same object as well as irregular arrangements of objects.

The Little Book of Colour, Shape and Number

Writing numerals

Focus: Mark making and number play

Steps along the way (stages of development of this concept):

- Draw lines and circles.
- Understand marks convey meaning.
- Recognise numerals; use number names in play and everyday situations.
- Engage in simple pretend play.
- Use mark making and props as part of sequences of simple pretend play and role-play.

Early Learning Goals:

CLL: engage in activities requiring hand-eye coordination; draw lines and circles using gross motor movement; begin to use anticlockwise movement and retrace vertical lines

MD: say and use number names in order in familiar contexts; recognise numerals 1 to 9; use mathematical language in play

Key skills and concepts:

- know marks convey meaning
- engage in role-play
- use a pencil effectively to draw circles and lines
- attempt to write numerals

Key words:

- number words
- less
- different
- more
- same

The Little Book of Colour, Shape and Number

Ten ideas to get you started:

- Make cardboard replica mobile phones and phone cards. Add Post-it notes and telephone books for recording numbers.
- Gather together lots of junk mail forms and envelopes. Open the junk mail together, filling in forms with numbers and marks. Look for numbers and familiar letters.
- Roll a dice, count the spots and record the numeral. Encourage all attempts at mark making.
- Set up a catalogue shop role-play with tills, order forms to complete and numbers to copy out from catalogues.
- Make price labels for shop play.
- Set up a woodwork role-play with rulers and tapes, pencils and wood and so on. Play together measuring the wood and furniture and drawing pictures, adding pretend measurements and so on.
- Build towers of stacking beakers and bricks. Mark numerals on sticky labels and fix to the beakers in order.
- Make tiny number plates for toy cars, and pretend tax discs for bikes and pedal cars outside.
- Make junk model phones and calculators, adding numbers.
- Use icing sugar pens to add numbers to plain biscuits. Decorate with a matching number of icing sugar stars.

Taking it further:

- Cut out different clock shapes, adding the numbers and hands. Hold punch the clock faces and weave wool and ribbon in and out of the holes, talking about the numbers and times of the day.

Look and listen:

- Listen for children using number names in play and counting independently.
- Observe how children hold pens and pencils.
- Look for children using vertical and horizontal lines in their mark making as well as marking a circle.
- Watch how children intend to record and convey information with their mark making.

The Little Book of Colour, Shape and Number

Working with parents

Working together

Maths in the foundation stage is about experiencing, learning practising and using mathematical concepts and language in everyday play situations and routines. Young children learn best from the familiar and things that are of particular significance to them. Before they embark on the foundation stage they will already have begun to develop early mathematical knowledge and make mathematical discoveries about the world, such as:

- stacking and nesting beakers and bricks;
- recognising lots of cars, or just a few;
- discovering that objects are the same and different;
- practising full and empty, and 'all gone';
- learning first number names, in simple finger, nursery and tickle rhymes, such as 'Round and Round the Garden Like a Teddy Bear'.

Every child will have had a different range of experiences before starting in your setting. These may have been at home, with other carers or in other settings. Sharing the knowledge of what has happened before and using this to inform planning is a great way to get off to a really good start in your partnership with parents. Help parents to know what is happening in the setting to develop their child's mathematical knowledge by:

- making a statement in your prospectus or brochure;
- making sure all resources are clearly labelled with what they are and what they are used for - for example, on the beads note that they are used for threading, counting, making patterns, sorting;
- talking to parents about why you have planned activities;
- creating a bulletin for parents which explains what you are doing to help their child's early maths, and include some ideas that parents could try at home;
- putting up a poster with some of your maths resources, explaining what maths is about in the foundation stage;
- display some photos of the children doing maths activities.

Using treasure baskets for colour, shape and number

Make collections of interesting natural and everyday objects around a theme such as a shape, or number objects, or perhaps a colour give children a chance to develop language skills, explore new ideas or concepts and practise fine motor skills. Why not organise a workshop or information session for parents about treasure baskets and together develop treasure basket collections to loan, or offer lists of objects for parents to collect for their children.

A treasure basket to explore colours might include:
- rainbow coloured gloves and socks;
- spotty and stripy fabric;
- pictures of rainbows;
- coloured cellophane and flimsy scarves to peer through;
- coloured plastic lenses on sunglasses;
- transparent objects to look through;
- pieces of tissue and cellophane to lay over each other to mix colours.

You could also try treasure basket colour themes of:
- black and white;
- spots or stripes;
- single colours and their shades;
- textures;
- silver and gold;
- transparent objects.

A treasure basket to explore shape might have round things in it (spheres, tubes, circles, discs), and might include:
- balls of different sizes, shapes and textures;
- CDs;
- an orange;
- some round beads;
- coins;
- marbles;
- plates;
- jar lids;
- corks;
- tubes;
- buttons.

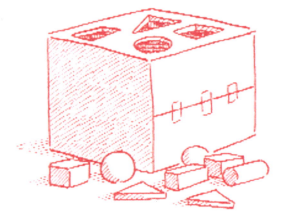

You could also try treasure basket shapes themes of:
- rectangles and cuboids;
- squares and cubes;
- triangles, cones, diamonds and stars;
- large and small versions of the same shapes;
- spirals.

A treasure basket to explore number might include:

- telephones;
- calculators;
- rulers;
- price labels;
- clocks with numerals;
- purse with coins;
- telephone number book;
- birthday cards with numbers on;
- library cards;
- plastic or wooden numerals;
- wooden and plastic numbers;
- magnetic numbers;
- little bags, boxes, tins for collections of small objects;
- number labels, stickers.

You could also try treasure basket number themes of:

- groups of three or five objects in little zip lock bags and purses including coins, beads, sequins, little bricks, counters;
- pairs of matching objects;
- groups of objects for counting, such as candles on a cake; basket of apples, keys on a ring, pennies in a purse, bricks in a tower.

The Little Book of Colour, Shape and Number

Maths ideas for every day, at home, in your setting, out and about.

Everyday life with young children offers endless opportunities to make learning about colour, shape and number fun and immediate. Here are just a few ideas to get you started.

Colours

- Play 'I Spy' by colour, perhaps 'I spy with my little eye something red'.
- Go on a hunt for different patterns.
- Matching and sorting socks and washing, talking about colours and patterns.
- On a visit to the supermarket or shops, tick off colours from a list as you find them.
- Guess the colour of the next car to come round the corner or past the garden fence.

Shapes

- Spot five triangles as you walk around the streets or park, then five circles and then five squares.
- Make patterns together with cutlery - spoon, fork, spoon, fork etc.
- Talk about everyday objects and their shapes.
- Find shapes on buildings. Look at an interesting building together as you walk along the street. What shapes can you see? Look at windows, doors, bricks, steps.
- Make sandwiches of different shapes and arrange them in different patterns on the plate.

Numbers

- Let children help to dial or press numerals on phones, television remote controls, calculators, computers.
- Spot numbers on registration plates. 'Can we spot a number 3?'
- Count steps and stairs together.
- Count out spoons, cups and plates as you get out or put away the lunch or dinner things.
- Count how many people are waiting at the bus stop. Guess how many more passengers will get on the bus.

Number rhymes, songs and games

Ask parents to share favourite games with you. Collect songs, rhymes and games they remember from their own childhood.

Some rhymes and songs to start your collection:

- There Were Ten in the Bed;
- Baa Baa Black Sheep;
- When Goldilocks Went to the House of the Bears;
- Five Elephants Went Out to Play;
- When I was One, I ate a Bun the day I went to sea;
- Hickory, Dickory Dock;
- Peter Hammers With one Hammer;
- Ten Fat Sausages;
- Five Currant Buns in the Bakers Shop;
- The Animals Went in Two by Two;
- Two Little Dickie Birds;
- Five Little Speckled Frogs;
- Five Fat Peas in a Pea Pod Pressed;
- One Potato, Two Potato;
- Five Little Leaves So Bright and Gay;
- One Man Went to Mow;
- One, Two Three, Four, Five, Once I Caught a Fish Alive;
- One, Two Three, Four, Mary at the Cottage Door;
- Round and Round the Garden Like a Teddy Bear.

There are so many rhymes to choose from one. These are just some of our favourites. Why not add puppets, instruments (real or improvised), clapping or actions, soft toys as props.

Choose a few favourites and make a poster, a list with the words and actions, or a photo book of the children singing and playing them for parents to take home and enjoy with their child.

If you have found this book useful you might also like ...

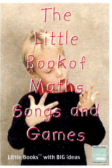

The Little Book of Maths Songs & Games
LB12
ISBN 1-904187-32-3

The Little Book of Maths Activities
LB11
ISBN 1-904187-08-0

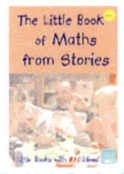

The Little Book of Maths from Stories
LB40
ISBN 1-905019-25-4

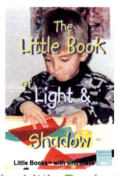

The Little Book of Light & Shadow
LB25
ISBN 1-904187-81-1

All available from

Featherstone Education   PO Box 6350
Lutterworth   LE17 6ZA
T:0185 888 1212   F:0185 888 1360
on our web site
www.featherstone.uk.com
and from selected
book suppliers